CONTENTS

Excellent employment . . . on a Shoestring

Hiring the best people to help your business grow

Ann Andrews

A & C Black

First published in New Zealand by Reed Publishing (NZ) Ltd, 2004
as *Did I Really Employ You?*

First published in Great Britain 2007

A & C Black Publishers Ltd
38 Soho Square, London W1D 3HB
www.acblack.com

British Library Cataloguing in Publication Data
A CIP record for this book is available from the British Library.

ISBN: 978-0-7136-8210-6

This book is produced using paper that is made from wood grown in
mnaged, sustainable forests. It is natural, renewable and recyclable.
The logging and manufacturing processes conform to the environ-
mental regulations of the country of origin.

Design by Fiona Pike, Pike Design, Winchester
Typeset by RefineCatch Limited, Bungay, Suffolk
Printed in Italy by Rotolito

CONTENTS

To Marj, Ron and Flo, my very special people.

ACKNOWLEDGEMENTS

I have been running creative recruitment workshops for a number of years, both in-house and as public workshops. A question I was frequently asked is: 'Where can I find a book on creative recruiting?'

The answer was usually, 'I'm not sure.' There were dozens of recruitment books in the shops, but they seemed to be written mainly from the applicant's point of view, rarely from that of the interviewer. So I decided to convert my workshop into such a book.

As the manuscript became thicker and thicker, my little printer couldn't cope with the sheer volume of pages, so every couple of days, I would pop down to my local copy shop, print off the manuscript, and call in at the various cafés in my area to check and edit and muse.

Thank you to Nick at MBE Newmarket; thanks also to Anton who owns Café Monet and manages to recruit the best employees ever. The biggest thanks, though, go to my partner Warren, because when my writing urge arrives, my cooking urge disappears. He makes sure we are well fed during the process.

AUTHOR'S NOTE

It's important for me to stress what this book is, and what it isn't.

This book is a 10-step process which can be used at any level of an organisation. It is designed primarily for 'front-end' positions, those that involve the eventual post-holder working with customers, clients, suppliers and so on.

The process will also work for team leader/manager and senior manager positions, but when recruiting people at these levels I always advise the additional step of using psychometric testing. Yes, it costs money, but, as will be seen in Part II, recruiting the wrong person will inevitably cost more.

This book is not, nor should it be considered, a 'legislative' process of recruiting. Each country has its own laws governing the employee/employer relation-ship, and because this legislation is constantly evolving, I strongly suggest that you run all your employment policies and documentation, including applications forms, past a specialist regularly. It will save you many headaches (and potentially a lot of money!) along the way. If are based in the UK, your solicitor would be a useful source of information, but you can also look online at:

- Business Link: www.businesslink.gov.uk
- Acas: www.acas.org.uk
- HM Revenue and Customs: www.hmrc.gov.uk

INTRODUCTION

We've all done it. Hired someone who, on the day of the interview seemed absolutely perfect for the job, then two months, two weeks or even two days after they start working for you, you begin asking the question 'Did I really employ you?'

The computer industry has a wonderful expression – garbage in, garbage out – meaning that the information you get out of your computer will only ever be as good as the information you put into it. People are the same.

The wonderfully motivated person you talked to on the day of the interview, who has now become an unreliable, lazy, half-hearted, clock-watcher, didn't actually metamorphose – he or she was actually an unreliable, lazy person to begin with.

The question is: Why did we not discover that at the interview?

I have interviewed hundreds of people in my years as a personnel and human resources manager and have made many, many mistakes. Initially I took people at face value and trusted that what they were telling me was the truth. I believed every word they said when they answered my carefully prepared interview questions.

It was only much later in my interviewing career that I realised people were often telling me only what they thought I wanted to hear. Maybe they were desperate for a job; perhaps they were just sick of going along to interviews that led nowhere. Whatever their rationale, I decided I had to get better at this recruiting thing. The employment contract is a bit like a marriage, easy to get into, but very time-consuming and costly to get out of.

In this book I will share with you some of the skills and tools I picked up over the years; it will help you to short-circuit some of the pain and trauma of recruiting square pegs and then trying to fit them into round holes.

The world of business is changing daily and recruiting the right people for the right job is no longer as straightforward as it once was. What we once classed as 'work' (manual) or career (for life) has changed beyond all recognition. When recruiting, we now need to be smarter to be sure the square pegs fit in square holes and the round pegs in round holes.

Employees have changed, too. They no longer want or expect jobs for life. The employment relationship is now a much shorter affair and it's vital that we find the right people first time so that we can maximise their short stay with us.

The whirlwind of today's commercial environment — and the high-pressure, long-hours effort required to get a small business off the ground — requires business owners and managers to spend their time working *on* their company, not just *in* it. And in order to do that, they must be able to hand over much of the basic, day-to-day decision-making to their employees.

It sounds simple, but it's not necessarily easy, particularly if the employees we have recruited only want to do as much as they have to — and no more. To be able to delegate the day-to-day running of a business to employees we need to recruit people who not only have the skills and potential ability to do the job, but also the attitude that says, 'I want to learn as much as I can every day I come to work.'

We must also leave behind the hierarchical, parent/child relationships that many organisations seem to foster (and then bitterly complain about), and move on to a more modern, adult/adult workplace. This may require us to recruit people who are better qualified than us, people who may question and challenge us. Once again, this is not an easy thing for some of us to do, particularly if we've started a business from nothing and ploughed all our hard-earned cash into it, not to mention 18 hours' hard graft a day.

In a fast-changing world, we need and expect our staff (and managers, if we have them) to become coaches and mentors, facilitators and educators — a tall order for those who have probably never encountered those responsibilities in their own working lives!

Whatever the size of a business, employers can expend an awful lot of energy on the whingers and whiners, or those people who don't want to be anything other than 'quit-and-stay' employees (the body shows up most days but the heart, soul and passion are left at home). So if you have a track record of recruiting these less-than-exciting people, and really want to recruit flexible, go-the-extra-mile employees, you will need to learn how to interview and select differently.

You will have to acquire special skills to get beyond the façade the employee is presenting, to ask the kind of questions that will reveal the real person. You will need to discover why they are sitting in front of you today, and the real skills and attributes they bring to the mix, not what they think you want to hear.

Employees have a responsibility in this transaction too. The modern workforce has to be flexible, accountable and willing to make decisions. Some people thrive in such an environment; others will do everything within their power to resist more responsibility (the child part of the parent/child equation) and then complain about decisions that have been made for them, even though they were asked to be involved in the decision-making process in the first place, but declined.

During my research for this book, I saw shelves and shelves of books dedicated to 'getting the job'. One book even had on its cover: 'say the right things to get that job'. Wouldn't it serve both parties' interests better to answer the questions honestly, so that rather than saying the right things, you get the right job?

All human resources managers have made mistakes and recruited the wrong people, and most people have made the mistake of taking on the wrong job. A position which sounded great on paper can, within a very short space of time, turn out to be an absolute nightmare. I've done it myself: I once took on a job which was supposedly a research technician; it turned out the job was actually a filing clerk in a research library! I lasted six weeks, bored out of my brain.

The knowledge that you may now have to spend the next two years (or however long you think is an appropriate time to have on your CV before you go through the whole horrendous process again) working in yet another boring job, and/or working with yet another boss from hell is painful. So let me take you through the steps to ensure 'the right fit' for both parties. That way everyone involved in the recruitment process saves a good deal of time and heartache.

PART I

How fast the world is changing

In times of dramatic change, it is the learners who inherit the future. The learned usually find themselves in a world that no longer exists.

Brian Gibbs, *Unlimited*

HOW FAST THE WORLD IS CHANGING

Before I get onto the tips and techniques of good recruiting, I need to explain why recruiting is so challenging in the current business climate.

Once upon a time, if you advertised a job in your local newspaper, the greatest challenge would have been finding the time to sift through the 30-40 applications you received. Nowadays, there is little possibility of too many people applying for a position. For many small businesses in today's employment market, if four or five people of the right calibre apply you can consider yourself very lucky. Often companies advertise several times and get no suitable applicants at all.

When organisations are asked why they think that is, the most common reply is that there is a shortage of skills. And they are right — we do not have enough skilled people — but there is another, much bigger, reason for the dearth of applications.

Between *60 and 70 million* children were born in the year to 18 months after the end of World War II. We know this generation as the 'baby boomers', and they're now in their early 60s.

To balance things up, the advent of the contraceptive pill in the 1960s saw that, within a year to 18 months of its introduction, an estimated *15 to 20 million* children were born (the baby bust!). The birth rate has never again risen to those dizzy post-war heights. If you do the maths, it doesn't take a rocket scientist to work out that the reason why not many people are applying for positions is that the bulge has moved on and there are no longer as many job-seekers out there.

So what we are facing is not just a shortage of skills, (though that is still relevant) but a worldwide shortage of people! For the first time ever, Europe, the traditional exporter of people, is now importing people with the skills and expertise required to maintain production levels.

The implications are immense. We live in what the business author and guru Tom Peters once referred to as a 'nanosecond world', where massive changes happen overnight. If we want to stay in business, we have to not only respond to these changes, but turn them into a competitive advantage before anyone else does.

Ongoing, never-ending training

Alongside demographic variations are the continuous and sometimes massive technological advances that are constantly occurring. The knock-on effect of these advances is the never-ending need to train and retrain staff. We tend to calculate the cost of this in purely financial terms, but frequently overlook the stress to staff that the continual need to increase skills, and the consequent high turnover rate, create.

The traditional way of recruiting was to look for people who already had the required skills, because it saved some of the costs of training. Unfortunately, because of the speed at which technology moves, many of those skills quickly become obsolete, and if the person we recruited had a marginal attitude, we now have two problems — a person with yesterday's skills who is resistant to learning anything new.

Recruiting for skills alone is no longer the best option. More than ever we need to recruit people who are willing to be life-long learners, who want to grow and develop, who want a career, not just a 'job'. And as if that isn't enough, businesses of all sizes now also need to find creative ways to look after the people they already have, because if key people leave it may not be easy to replace them.

> **TIP 1**
>
> When a person hands in their notice, offering them more money is only a short-term, quick-fix solution. Money is rarely the reason people leave. More money may appease them for a little while, until the real reason they were unhappy surfaces again (usually in about three months' time). Then what?

Today, we are also facing different sets of values. Young people are no longer looking for the job-for-life that previous generations depended on. They have a shorter attention span, they need and want constant change. To get the best from them and their energy, business owners and team leaders must be aware of the requirements of the younger workforce and be willing to provide more movement and stimulation.

Today's youth have been raised in the 'instant' world of the consumer society. If they don't get the stimulation they need, they are much more inclined to job-hop than any generation before them – and they don't seem to care what this looks like on their CV.

Oldies can be useful, too

The world has an ageing population, healthier than any generation before them. As employers and managers, we need to review our attitudes to age and maturity. Yes, a 50+ or 60+ person may be a bit slower than a 20+ person, but there are advantages in hiring older people: they have a wealth of experience, they're used to the rigours of work, and they are more likely to be permanently settled in an area and, therefore, willing to stay longer. A blend of young and mature is certainly worth considering, especially in the younger days of your business when you're trying to balance out energy and enthusiasm with tangible results.

One glaring example of the shortage of skilled people is in the health sector. Britain, Australia and New Zealand are all facing an acute shortage of nurses and that statistic is not likely to improve as retirement looms for many existing staff: the Royal College of Nursing estimated that in 2006, the average age of nurses in the UK was 42! Young women are resistant to taking on the role because of the length of training required and the poor salary they can expect at the end of that training. Teaching is facing similar problems.

Career and lifestyle choices

Career choices are changing too, especially for women. There was a time when women had just three career choices:

1. nursing
2. secretarial work
3. teaching

But today's women can be, and do, whatever they want — and they are not afraid to. Why should they be? They also demand better conditions than earlier generations had to put up with.

Although 50% of the workforce is female, statistics show that women are walking away from the corporate world in droves and setting up their own businesses. They have always had to work harder to get the same recognition as their male counterparts, and they are no longer prepared to do this within traditional organisations. You may even be one of those women.

Children *or* a career was how it worked; now the challenge is balancing children *and* career. For the most part, the business world hasn't been very proactive in the way it addresses the changing role of women in the workplace. Large organisations could arrange for an in-house crèche, and smaller ones could negotiate a good rate for their female staff with a local nursery, yet how many of them have done so?

Men, too, are now wanting and demanding more time to spend with their young families. Businesses may have to get serious about factoring in flexible hours — early starts/early doors, term-time working, job share, and so on — for their employees, male and female.

There appears to be a shift in values now. Burnout is a recognised health issue today, and has even been found to have links to diabetes.

Estimates are that 10% of Britain's working popula- tion now works outside Britain. These are not the employees in their 20s enjoying a late 'gap year'; they are the 30+ people who are increasingly buying land on the Continent (where it is much cheaper than in Britain) so they can have a lifestyle and a life!

Head-hunting

There has always been keen competition for good people. Head-hunting is alive and well. Do you know which of your key players could be poached? Do you know what the market rate is for those people? Are you paying them enough? Pay is a contentious issue for all businesses, whatever their size, but obviously small companies generally don't have as much cash to spend on their employees as larger concerns. If you don't recruit carefully and look after your employees, though, how vulnerable is your business and the future of your business? When you lose people, you lose experience and shared knowledge too, and in a small company, sometimes you can't put too high a price on that.

The cost of staff turnover

There are wide variances on the estimated cost of staff turnover. Expert opinions vary between a starting point of around 75% of the annual salary for that position up to 24 times that person's salary!

There is a tendency for managers to think that the only investment required to find a new person is the cost of the advertisements and someone's time to interview the candidates. You will see how and why the costs can escalate to such an alarming degree if you factor in any of the following.

- The deterioration in the incumbent's productivity once she decides she wants out.
- The cost of her lost productivity once she starts sneaking out for interviews.
- The knowledge she may take with her once she goes.
- The clients that may follow her.

16

- The cost of retraining the new recruit.
- The time it takes to bring the new recruit up to the speed and productivity level of the previous job holder.
- The mistakes the new recruit will (inevitably) make until he or she is up to speed.

As you can see, there are plenty of hidden recruitment costs. If your business is big enough to have a human resources department or officer, you may also now see why they give you such a hard time whenever you ask them to recruit another new person!

TIP 2

A comfortable regenerative level for staff turn-over is 2–7%.

As the business owner or manager, you are accountable for your company's bottom line and if the company has a high staff turnover (or 'churn' rate), you now have a very strong business motivator for getting this recruiting thing right.

The good news about turnover

Having looked at the bad news about recruitment and its costs, let's look at the good news. The fact is that *some* staff turnover can be healthy, even in a small or relatively new business. Every now and then we need fresh blood, fresh thinking and an injection of energy or knowledge.

When I first work with a new team, I ask each person how long he or she has been with that particular company. We then add all those years of service together. It can sometimes add up to several hundred years of wisdom and tradition, pride and experience.

My quiet thought when someone tells me they have 15 years' experience is often, 'Ah yes, but is that really 15 years' experience or one year's experience repeated 15 times?' Long tenure can be an organisation's greatest strength; the paradox is that it can also be its greatest weakness!

At this stage I always ask the newest people in the team if they noticed anything when they first arrived which to them looked ridiculous. Hardly anyone ever answers me of course . . . I may get a few embarrassed titters or nervous coughs, but gradually people start to see the point I am making, which is that when a new person joins, especially if they come from a different industry, they are the best person to answer that question. They have no preconceived ideas, no learned habits, and they haven't yet put on the company blinkers.

If a new person dares to ask an existing employee why they do things a certain way, they will almost without fail be given one of three stock answers:

1. 'We've always done it that way', or
2. 'That is how you do it', or worse still
3. 'Who are you and what do you know about anything? You've only been here five minutes!'

Even in small businesses, this is the organisational mind-set. Which is a great shame, because if we were willing to ask our new recruits what they see us doing that looks ridiculous, and if we were then courageous enough to go one step further and make it safe for them to let us know, not only might we learn something, we might actually be able to make some major improvements.

It is true that greatest leaps forward in thinking rarely come from inside an industry. They usually come from outside, from a person who says, 'Why do you do it that way?' or 'I think I can show you a faster/cheaper way to do that.'

PART II

Pre-interview

WHAT YOU CAN DO PRE-INTERVIEW

If a vacancy arises at your company, some time spent doing a job analysis *before* you decide to advertise can save you many hours of unnecessary interviewing, and many thousands of pounds. And it will help you to avoid employing the wrong kind of person, or even advertising the wrong job!

One company I worked for had an incredibly high turnover of telemarketing staff: average tenure was a mere three months! When we started conducting exit interviews to investigate the reasons why, we discovered that we were recruiting 'sales' people, when in fact what we really needed in this position was good customer service people – a very different skills set altogether.

> **TIP 3**
>
> Always conduct exit interviews with employees who are leaving, preferably after the people have been paid and they have been given their references. You will be amazed at what you will discover if you make it safe for them to be honest.

Once we realised this, we adjusted the requirements for the position and recruited a different type of person. Turnover was stemmed and our customers were much happier. So before you rush into recruiting a new person, try the following exercise.

Job analysis — why do you need this position?

> **TIP 4**
>
> Ask the question: Do we need to replace at all?

Ask yourself:

1. What is the purpose of the job (results to be achieved)?

2. Are these results still relevant in today's climate?
3. Is there a better way to achieve these results?
4. Do we need to replace at all?
5. Can we simplify the job and use the money saved to do something else?
6. Do the tasks/responsibilities offer possibilities to promote internally, thereby creating a career opportunity for someone else?
7. Can we use this opportunity to design a completely new position to cover the aspects of our team which we are currently lacking?
8. Can we combine this job with another to give someone a more interesting role?
9. Can we then use the space created to bring in a completely different set of skills?
10. Would it be more effective to outsource this job?

And finally, a very creative question to ask: *Is the job already completed?*

If you look very closely, you may discover that some of the jobs in your business are being done simply because they have always been done; or worse, that they are done in a certain way because they have always been done in a certain way.

Put *everything* under the microscope. Question the status quo and let your team know that you want them to question it too. Give people an incentive to get rid of unnecessary detail. After all, people will only do what they are rewarded for; if they are rewarded for just going through the motions, they will. If, however, they are rewarded to find better ways to do things, they will.

> To illustrate, the international courier company, Federal Express, was experiencing a problem — no matter how many systems and controls management created, they were still having difficulty getting parcels and planes out on time. In the words of Fred Smith, the CEO:
>
> *It became obvious that the underlying problem was that it was in the interests of the employees at cargo terminal — college kids mostly — to run late, because it meant that they made more money. So what we did was give them all a minimum guarantee [of a base wage] and said, 'Look, if you get through by a certain time, you can go home early.'*
>
> Ann Andrews, *Shift Your But*
>
> Suddenly, packages and planes went out on time.

Fred Smith also said that he didn't think it was a conscious decision by the employees to go slow: they weren't out to 'get' the company; it just served their financial needs to make the job fill the hours they were going to get paid for.

So how do you measure a job well done? Firstly, examine error rates. Look at the targets people are given (particularly people doing administrative tasks). Then measure the output. What is the end result you require? Are you getting it?

TIP 5

Reed, one of the UK's leading recruitment specialists, estimated that it costs roughly £5,000 to hire a new member a staff. So before a new employee even starts working for you, and long before they start producing, you are already considerably out of pocket. So the question 'Do we need to replace at all?' makes at the very least £5,000 worth of good business sense.

Review standards regularly. Better still, encourage your staff to review them.

A comment that is frequently heard when working with teams is that their boss or managers are 'always shifting the goalposts'. My response to that is: 'Great. Be pleased that your company is sufficiently on the ball that it does so. Imagine what would happen if they didn't – within a very short space of time your company would be defunct and you'd be out of work.'

Don't be afraid to ask your employees: 'Now that we have achieved x, what do we need to do to achieve y?' If you offered your staff 10% of any savings they found or of any productivity improvements they made, those savings and improvements would happen overnight! However, you must realise that it won't be possible to keep asking your staff for more, better, and quicker without them eventually wanting to see a reward.

Mistakes people make in recruitment

If a valued member of staff hands in their notice and cannot be persuaded to stay, the first mistake you can make is to rush out and put an ad in the newspaper. The second mistake is to advertise exactly the same job as was being performed by the person who is leaving!

> **TIP 6**
>
> Ask the question: How could we better use the money saved?

A much better course of action would be to take some time to consider the incredible opportunities for your business presented by a person about to leave, sad as that may be on a personal level.

When working with teams, I always ask team members, 'On a scale of 1–10, how bored are you?' (1 being bored out of your mind, 10 being perfectly happy). Most managers are horrified when I show them the results — about 60–80% of employees fall into the 'bored-out-of-my-mind' category. What a waste! And what an opportunity!

Before you rush to advertise, set aside some time with anyone whose job may be affected by your staff member leaving. Ask them, the people on the front line, the biggest question of all: 'If we could save this salary, how could we better use the money to make your jobs easier, bearing in mind that we still have to maintain or improve our financial performance?'. And don't just pay lip service to this exercise, either: these are the people who will be steadying the ship once their colleague has left, so really tune in to what they're saying.

> ### TIP 7
>
> You could offer the salary of the person who is leaving to the team they have been working with. Suggest to them that they find a better way to use that money, while still getting that person's job done and still achieving or (even better) improving the team's targets. You will be amazed at the ideas and suggestions they will come up with.

Job descriptions

I've always had mixed feelings about job descriptions, mainly because, as the human resources person, I was the one who had to write them, and so often, before the ink was even dry, the job description would be out of date.

Yes, people need to know what the basic job entails and what results they are required to achieve when they apply for an advertised position, but because everything in our lives is changing so rapidly, a job description does need to be a 'living' document.

Employers try to capture the fact that the job description will need to constantly evolve as the business itself does, or as the general commercial climate changes, by adding phrases like 'and any other duties that the position requires', but what does that actually mean? And how do you measure the output of something so vague?

I prefer a document which states: 'The key responsibilities of the position are . . . The results that need to be achieved are . . . But this is a living document; other tasks and responsibilities can and will become part of the position as market forces change.'

This should not be a licence to dump any old rubbish tasks on your staff. A good employer will always look for people who have that can-do attitude, are prepared to go the extra mile, and who want to learn and grow.

I also prefer job descriptions that favour the collective output of the team or department, rather than the output of an individual, because this encourages a person who has finished their job or task to help out another team member who may be swamped or struggling. It is the *overall* result of the team or department that is critical.

Skills vs attitude – the 80/20 principle

> *I ask people who know American business well to name three or four chief executives who really made a difference. Not short term, but people who really sustained superb performance. Almost never does anybody mention a Harvard MBA, let alone any MBA.*
>
> Henry Mintzberg, Professor of Management,
> McGill University

Mintzberg addresses what I believe is the fundamental principle of recruitment – you need 20% skills and 80% attitude. For example, if you have a person in your team with a negative attitude, it will take approximately five positive people to overcome their energy!

Yes, we need a person with the right skills to do the job, but even at senior levels of the business (in fact, especially at the senior levels) we need the right skills plus a great attitude.

For example, a busy manager is down to the last two candidates for a position. One has the perfect skills and is able to start straight away, but is brash and arrogant; the other doesn't yet have all the skills required but has an amazing 'can-do' attitude. Which candidate should the manager choose?

The answer is always the person with attitude. Yet in real life, most managers would select the candidate with the skills because there would be little or no training required; he or she can apply their skills immediately.

The problem is what might happen in the long term. If there is an attitude problem, it will surface sooner or later and it will cost the company further down the track. By far the better solution is to take the person with the great attitude and be willing to invest the time and training to bring them up to speed.

TIP 8

The New Zealand Employment Court recently awarded an employee $40,000 (roughly £15,000) in back pay because he was a Seventh Day Adventist (whose Sabbath is Saturday) and the company had required him to work the occasional Saturday.

In the UK, you must not discriminate against a candidate on the grounds of religion. It is well worth taking specialist legal advice if you are at all unsure of current practice.

The application form – an amazing time-saving tool

Always ask candidates who are applying for positions at the lower levels of the organisation to complete an application form. Yes, invite people to send in their CVs, but e-mail, post or fax an application form to them as well. This gives you the opportunity to gather vital information before you even start the interviewing process.

Here are some examples of questions to ask people on the application form:

This position requires flexibility of hours. Are there any reasons why this may not be possible for you?

This industry works seven days per week, 24 hours per day. Is there any reason why working weekends and/or flexi hours would be a problem for you?

Note also, that as an employer you can highlight specific medical conditions on the application form that should be declared if considered relevant in your industry:

This job requires that you lift heavy packages. Do you have any conditions or disabilities likely to be aggravated by doing this?

This business operates in the food industry. Do you have any known health problems which would prevent you from fulfilling the duties of this position?

The legislation designed to protect the rights of the individual is a minefield. However, as an employer there are certain things you need to know about a prospective employee before you recruit. So how do you deal with the tricky areas?

This position will occasionally require you to work overtime with little notice. Could this be a problem for you?

This position requires that you train in other areas of the department. Is there any reason why this would be unacceptable to you?

Are you legally entitled to work in the UK?

If 'yes', is this by virtue of citizenship, permanent residency or a work permit? If you are invited to the next stage of interviews, we would require you to bring proof of this with you.

You are able to ask, and candidates are required to answer, questions that are relevant to the position. Any deliberate untruths by the employee which are uncovered later may justify dismissal.

For a position at the team leader/middle manager level (once again, only if relevant) you may need to ask questions such as the following:

> This position requires a certain amount of travel and that could mean you being away from home for short periods of time. Is there any reason why this would be a problem for you?

Also go through the application form with a fine-tooth comb. Look for things like:

- continuity of employment (check the gaps)
- reasons for leaving various positions (these will need to be verified when checking references). Is there a pattern?

Request permission to keep the application form on file, remembering that, to be in line with the Data Protection Act, the information on the application form cannot be given to anyone else (other than a government agency) or used for any other purpose, without the employee's permission. For extra help on this issue, visit the Information Commissioner's website (**www.ico.gov.uk**) or ring the helpline on 08456 30 60 60.

General questions

Here are some general questions which will encourage people to open up:

- What are the things that stress you, and how do you manage those stressors?
- What motivates you to do your best work?
- What aspects of your previous jobs did you like the most?
- What management style are you most comfortable with?
- What management style are you least comfortable with?
- What are the qualities you believe you bring to this job?
- Tell me about the worst co-worker you have ever had and why were they so bad?
- What excited you about this position?
- What is the greatest obstacle you have had to overcome in your life?
- What has been your greatest achievement?

> **TIP 9**
>
> The more information you have about the job, about the ideal person for the job and the ideal fit for the organisation with regard to where it is going rather than where it has been, the better decision you will be able to make in selecting the best person for the job.

And two questions I think every candidate for every position should be asked are:

- Do you have any additional skills or attributes that we haven't explored which may be of relevance to the position or useful for the company?
- What do you know about this company?

If the prospective recruit hasn't taken any time at all to find out about the company, what does that tell you? If they're not interested in you, why should you be in them? On the other hand, there are people who go too far. They will have found out everything about the company from the date it was formed to the flavour of the CEO's favourite toothpaste. Look for a balance.

Use only one or two of these general questions at the very most, carefully choosing the most appropriate for the position you are advertising. Remember, the main point of such questions is to get the person talking about themselves.

If it is obvious that the person is totally unsuitable, end the interview as quickly and respectfully as you can, by saying something like: 'We are simply doing quick face-to-face interviews at the moment and plan to contact those people we would like to come back for a more in-depth interview. Thank you for your time; I will be in touch over the next few days.' And then do get in touch.

When interviewing, it is important that you stick to times and dates. Also make sure that while you are interviewing you will not be disturbed. Small businesses often don't have vast amounts of space to play with, but you should conduct the interview somewhere quiet and private. Tell your colleagues that you'll be interviewing between 10 and 1 (say), divert your landline to reception or your voicemail and turn your mobile phone off. Once the candidates have arrived, it's also courteous to ask them whether they mind if you take notes. Remember that they do have the right to see those notes at a later date, if they so wish.

Never, during the interview, give a person the impression that they have been successful in securing the position, no matter how well they come across. This can be quite tricky just in terms of verbal constructions, as it's easier (and more of a reflex) to say 'you' when we mean 'the eventual post-holder' or 'the successful candidate'. They are a bit of a mouthful, yes, but it's worth being very clear on this issue. Even if the first person you interview that day gives a knock-out performance, it is still possible that you may change your mind or a better applicant could come along further down the list. See everyone before you even begin to evaluate. First impressions can be wrong.

I always like to spend a few minutes between interviews to summarise my thoughts on the applicant. Interviewing is a bit like house-hunting — after a while, the houses start to blur, so schedule in some time (15 minutes, say) between candidates so that you can collect your thoughts and take a quick break.

INTERVIEWING SCHOOL LEAVERS

School leavers can present a real challenge because, obviously, they have had no previous experience in the workplace. The best way to handle interviews with them is to adapt the 'manager' questions to 'teacher' and to ask them to talk about projects they have completed, or holiday jobs they have had. Checking references is still important.

Ending the interview

It is often a good idea to end the interview with a light-hearted, more relaxed question. Questions like these will tell you much about the interviewee's values. But ask only one:

- If you could spend a day with a famous person (living or dead), whom would you choose?
- If you won £5 million, what would you do differently?
- If you were elected prime minister, what would be the first thing you would do when taking up office?

And my favourite:

- What would your best friend say is your most irritating trait?

I have found out more about a person by asking this simple question than all the other questions put together.

For example, I was interviewing for a middle manager several years ago and the 'irritating trait' question was the last thing I asked every applicant. Most people answered without any apparent difficulty, but two people stood out that day.

One man became very defensive. He sat straight up in his chair, flushed bright red, became very hot under the collar and actually said, 'I have difficulty with such a non-relevant question', to which I replied, 'That's fine, let's not pursue it.'

Later that day I asked another man the same question. He burst out laughing. He said 'I have no idea but I'll go home and ask my wife — no doubt she will enlighten me!'

The next day he called me and told me the question had been the catalyst for the most interesting dinner-time conversation they had had in a long time.

As it turned out, neither man got the job in the end, but if I had been forced to choose between these two men as the only candidates, I know which of them I would have employed.

It's all about attitude and being willing to laugh at your own inadequacies. After all, we all have them.

TIP 10

An optimist is someone who finds an opportunity in every difficulty. A pessimist is someone who finds a difficulty in every opportunity.

Attracting the right person for the job

This will require you to go outside conventional recruitment processes. You could:

- Involve other members of your team to consider how an ideal candidate would think/act/behave.
- Involve those who will work directly with the new person.
- Analyse the current strengths and weaknesses of the team and then look for a person with the strengths that are lacking in the current team. (Sales teams are often lacking in detail/systems people; and accounting teams are often lacking in creative people.)
- Talk to a person who already does the job well. Ask them what are the skills and aptitudes they bring to the position and therefore the skills and aptitudes you need to look for.

Gather as much information as you can about the job. Decide what talents and skills the 'ideal' candidate would possess, and what (if any) extra skills would fit best with the organisation and the direction it is going. (Remember, we're looking forward now.) You will then be able to make better decisions and employ the best person for the job.

THE 12 SIGNS OF A BAD LISTENER

Part of being a successful interviewer is how good a listener you are. How do you rate? Take this test and see. Award yourself marks between 1 and 10 (1 being 'I do this all the time', 10 being 'I never do this').

Then get someone you know to check your response!

- ☐ I interrupt.
- ☐ I am thinking of my reply as you speak.
- ☐ I tend to change the subject in the middle of something you are saying.
- ☐ I have difficulty in answering direct questions.
- ☐ I tend to jump to conclusions.

- [ ] I tend to finish people's sentences.
- [ ] I tend to assume I know what you are going to say next.
- [ ] I tend to give advice.
- [ ] I feel the need to fill pauses.
- [ ] I shuffle a lot when people are talking to me.
- [ ] I try to fix people's problems.
- [ ] I can guarantee that whatever has happened to others has happened to me tenfold.

PART III

The 10-step process

THE 10-STEP RECRUITING PROCESS

We are now at the heart of how to do this 'recruiting thing' differently. I've boiled it down to the following 10 steps:

1. 'Designing' the ideal candidate
2. The value of a preliminary telephone interview
3. The formal vs the casual interview
4. The face-to-face interview
5. Negative factors to watch for during the interview
6. Final evaluation of the candidates
7. Creative confirmation
8. After the interviews
9. Checking references
10. Evaluating the process

Step 1 'Designing' the ideal candidate

To 'design' the ideal candidate you will need to ask yourself and/or some team members the following questions. The more people involved at this design stage, the better.

Q1   What do we already have in the existing job holder that we want to retain?

Q2   What we do not have at the moment that it would be an advantage to have in the future?

Q3   What do we have in the existing person that we absolutely don't want? (This is not about blame or giving the existing employee a hard time; instead it is about taking on board what you've learned since you recruited the current staff member and what skills you need now that you perhaps didn't need then.)

For example, if you're employing a receptionist, the answers to these questions might look like this.

A1 What we already have in our current receptionist:

■ a good telephone manner
■ good customer skills *most of the time*

A2 What we do not have now that we would like to have:

- Computer literacy
- The ability or willingness to do basic accounts
- The willingness to work flexible hours

A3 What we have that we really don't want:

- Poor time management
- Grumpiness

You will pick up on these characteristics later, when you design the interview.

Step 2 The value of a preliminary telephone interview

Because no-one wants to spend hours interviewing every candidate, it is important that during the first round of interviews you elicit the standard information as quickly and efficiently as possible. A phone interview is often the best way of doing this if you have lots of applicants, especially if you are looking to employ someone who, like the receptionist, will spend a lot of time on the telephone.

For example, the national sales manager for a home-care company with a fairly high turnover spends a good part of her time interviewing prospective candidates. She has a wonderful preliminary technique: she asks applicants to leave a short message on her answer-phone stating why they think she should employ them! It saves her hours of interviewing people who would be totally unsuitable.

Before you conduct a phone interview, make sure that you have:

■ completed the evaluation process and listed the things you are looking for in the ideal candidate
■ read each candidate's CV or application form

You will formulate your telephone questions based on this information. Allow 15 to 20 minutes for each candidate, keeping the interview short and sharp. Your goal is to ask a few key questions which will:

1. let the person know you want to know about them
2. uncover enough information to decide whether you want to invite this person to a more in-depth interview. For example:

> This vacancy is for a receptionist who has word processing skills and some basic accounting skills. Could you tell me about

your background and experience in each of these areas?

If you were to place the three skills — dealing with customers, typing and accounts — in order of preference, which category do you enjoy least?

This position requires some flexibility in your hours of work. Is there any reason why this would be unacceptable to you?

This position may occasionally require you to help out in other departments when they get busy. What are your thoughts on that?

Once you have gathered enough basic information to decide whether or not you want this person to go on to a face-to-face interview, end the call on a positive note, thanking them for their time and letting them know that you will be in touch if you need to call them in for an interview.

After the telephone interviews, once you've decided on the best applicants for the shortlist, it is essential that you send a note to the unsuccessful candidates. There is nothing worse than leaving people in limbo. Not only is it good manners to let people know the outcome, it is also good PR. Most of us talk about our job campaigns, and word will get around if people feel you've treated them badly. Also, you never know when you may need to advertise again. They may not have been right for this position, but they may be perfect for something else down the track.

> **TIP 11**
>
> In any interview, the answers you get are only as good as the questions you ask.

Don't ever promise what you have no intention of delivering either: waiting for the call, letter or e-mail that never arrives is painful and disheartening.

Step 3 Formal vs casual interviews

When designing a formal interview, it's absolutely vital that you:

- ask everyone the same questions, and
- ensure that all questions relate to the core competencies required for the position (which skills, attitude and team fit). Don't keep moving the goalposts in *this* situation.

This makes it easier to be objective and to evaluate the final candidates on facts rather than perception, or worse, to evaluate from an emotional perspective. If you fall into the trap of conducting casual interviews, then you will find that you create a situation which:

- takes the form of an informal conversation.
- asks different questions of each candidate, so each interview takes on a life and form of its own.
- places great emphasis on building rapport with the interviewer (which, if you are the interviewer, leads to recruiting a person in your own image!). You like the person, they seem to be on the same wavelength, and everyone gets that warm fuzzy feeling. The problem is they may not bring the complementary skills you need.
- is virtually impossible to evaluate logically or objectively.

In this scenario, because different questions are asked of different candidates, the interview becomes more about 'personality' than about the job, and more about whether you 'like each other', than about the ability to do the job and fit in with the culture of the organisation.

TIP 12

You can't listen if you are talking and if you are talking you will never learn anything.

Step 4 The face-to-face interview

If you are in the fortunate position of having many applicants, you will need a couple of interview phases. The first interview is designed for a brief look-see — perhaps 30–40 minutes with each candidate — followed closely by a second, more in-depth interview for the three or four people you feel are the best prospects.

You will have established from their application form and/or CV and the preliminary telephone interview whether the remaining applicants have the right match of skills you are looking for, so the face-to-face interview is better used to establish the attitude of the person. As much as you need someone with the right skills for the job, you also want a person who will contribute in areas where your team or organisation is weak. Remember the question:

> What do we not have now that we would like in the future?

During a trial face-to-face interview it is important that you do only about 50% of the talking. Yes, you need to give the applicant a brief overview of the company and the role, but the aim of this interview is to ask questions and then to sit back, listen and observe. How difficult can that be?

Obviously, you'll be listening closely to what candidates are saying and how they say it, but be alert to other clues too. Watch body language, reactions, comfort and discomfort, confidence and demeanour. However, what you observe should be measured in the context of the whole person – someone being interviewed for the first time is clearly going to have less confidence than a seasoned trooper.

TIP 13

If you are interviewing people from other cultures, don't place too much emphasis on eye contact. In some countries (particularly those in the Far East), not making eye contact is actually a mark of their respect for you. In other cases it could be a sign of youth or even shyness.

Now is the time to find out more about the character of

the person, their attitudes and responses to a variety of situations, their ability to fit into a team, their flexibility and willingness to grow and develop. Focus on only five to seven key areas — no-one is perfect!

Continuing with our example of the receptionist position, we decided that what we already had in our current receptionist was someone who:

- had a good telephone manner and
- had customer skills most of the time

> **TIP 14**
>
> The sole purpose of a job interview is to distinguish which person from a group of candidates is likely to succeed best in the job.

What we didn't have that we would now like to have was:

- computer literacy
- the ability or willingness to do basic accounts
- the willingness to work flexible hours

And what we had that we definitely didn't want was:

- poor time management
- grumpiness

You have saved valuable time by asking each candidate questions that cover some of these areas at the telephone interview stage. However, because you've decided that it's really important to have someone who can use a PC, it's a good idea to have them demonstrate their computer skills in front of you or a colleague.

Yes, they will be nervous, and this must be factored in to your assessment, but you will still be able to establish beyond doubt whether they can actually use the PC proficiently or not. Arrange to have them come in early to do this – perhaps set an office aside and have someone available to oversee the process.

With regard to the ability to do basic accounts, this is of course more difficult to ascertain unless they have appropriate qualifications. Verify when checking their references.

The skills and strengths we now need to establish at the face-to-face stage of the interviewing process are:

- people skills (customer service – internal and external)
- time management
- grumpiness

Which, if we now turn each into a positive, become:

- an excellent customer service attitude
- good time-keeping
- a cheerful disposition

And because we now want to gauge a prospective employee's 'attitude', we can add:

- a good team player
- initiative
- motivation

We are now ready to design the questions for the formal interview.

People skills (customer service — internal and external)
Some useful questions here might be:

> Tell me about a time when you had to deal with a particularly difficult co-worker. What happened, how did you handle the situation and what was the final outcome?

Or:

Customers can sometimes be incredibly demanding – tell me about a time when you had to deal with a difficult customer. How did you deal with the situation and what was the result?

Time management

What do you do if you find you are running late in the mornings?

Or:

On a scale of 1 to 10 (1 being terrible and 10 being perfect), how would you rate your time management skills?

Always check time management at the reference stage.

Cheerful disposition

What is the best part of the day for you? (Night owls may feel grumpy and un-cooperative in the mornings.)

Or:

What would you do if a co-worker offended you?

Or:

What coping strategies do you have for days when you are tired or under stress?

A good team player

What are your expectations of other team members and what do you think they might need from you?

Or:

What would you do if, five minutes before the end of your official working day, a co-worker asks you to do a job you know will take you a good half hour?

Initiative

Have you ever done a job which you knew you could have done more effectively? Tell me about the idea and let me know what you did to gain buy-in to the idea.

TIP 15

A person earning £25k per year who wastes one hour every day is costing the company

---

approximately £3,000 annually. And that's a conservative estimate when you factor in the cost of missed deadlines, failed promises and missed opportunities.

Motivation

What are your two- and five-year goals?

Or:

What motivates you to get things done?

Depending on the type of industry your business operates in, you may want to look at other attributes in your interviewing process. The following list is not exhaustive, but will give you a general feel for the questions you can ask to get behind the 'interview mask' in a friendly, non-threatening manner and extract a wealth of information about the candidate's attitude.

Listening and following instructions

When was the last time you made a mistake after someone had passed instructions to you? Talk me through. What happened?

Communication skills

Tell me about a time when someone passed on instructions to you and you misheard them? What was the outcome and how did you handle it?

A large part of this job requires you to pass on instructions – what is your preferred way of doing this?

Ability to learn quickly

I notice from your CV (or application form) that you took a Japanese language course at night school. Tell me how that went for you and what aspects you found the most challenging?

The power of asking 'Tell me about a time . . .' questions is that there is no right answer. It gets the person talking so that all you need to do is listen and observe, with the occasional 'oh' or 'that's interesting'.

Some interviewers either talk and talk and talk (and the interviewee gets to say very little), or they ask closed questions (where the only answer is yes or no). Both these strategies fail miserably to find out anything of value about the interviewee!

TIP 16

Remember to ask 'open' questions such as:

- Tell me about a time when you . . .
- Give me an example of . . .
- Talk me through how you would . . .

Step 5 Negative factors to watch for during the interview

- Poor personal appearance
- Inability to maintain eye contact
- Overbearing, aggressive, conceited people
- People who blame
- Overly passive people
- Overly agreeable people
- Those who can't express thoughts clearly — who waffle or go off on alarming tangents
- Lack of any interest or enthusiasm
- Lack of confidence
- Overemphasis on money, rewards, holidays and the like
- Lack of tact, maturity or courtesy
- Evasiveness
- Condemnation of past employers

■ Failure to ask you any questions
■ Discomfort when asked certain questions —
   this may require gentle probing to find out
   what is behind the reaction

Do keep all of the above in context, of course; one bad
trait does not suggest a murderer. However, if the person displays several of the above behaviours, it may be
cause for concern. Be alert.

Step 6 Final evaluation of the candidates

■ Review the information gathered for each
   applicant.
■ Rate each applicant (it is best to go through all
   the applications on the same day while you are
   in the same mood).
■ Weight behavioural requirements (which
   attributes are most essential, which are pretty
   important and which are nice-to-have?).

You may, at this stage, end up with two candidates who
reach the desired standard. Always take time to consider other creative ways of ensuring you select the right
person (see page 69).

The information you've gathered can be laid out in a
simple table. For example:

Candidate	Cheery disposition	Telephone skills	Customer service skills	Time-management skills	PC literacy	Basic accounting skills	Flexibility	Total
Liz Simpson	4	0	4	3	5	2	3	21
Jane Evans	3	4	3	3	5	4	3	25
Cathy Thomson	5	0	5	4	3	3	5	25

Rating = 0 (low) to 5 (high)

In this case, the two most suitable applicants appear to be Jane and Cathy. However, if we look more closely at their high scores and their low scores, a different picture emerges.

> **TIP 17**
>
> In order to earn more, you have to *learn* more.

Jane's high scores are her typing skills and, to a slightly lesser degree, her telephone and basic accounting skills; her low points appear to be her disposition and a lack of flexibility.

Cathy's high points are her cheerful disposition, her background in customer service and her flexibility. Her low points are her lack of telephone skills. Jane would be able to do the job straight away, but how would her disposition and flexibility affect the company in the long term?

Yes, it would be quicker and cheaper in the short term to employ Jane. And yes, it would be more expensive to train Cathy but in the long term you could be employing exactly the same type of person who is leaving – a person with some skills but a poor attitude. Is that what you really want?

Always recruit a person with a can-do attitude; in the long term it is much cheaper.

> **TIP 18**
>
> A gossip is someone who talks about others. A bore is someone who talks about themselves. A brilliant conversationalist is one who talks *to* you *about* you.

Step 7 Creative confirmation

- Jane may be simply bad at interviews. They are pretty stressful, as we all know. Before you make that final decision, consider asking both applicants back for a second interview. Be willing to go one step further and have both applicants spend a whole day working with the team. People can and will be on their best behaviour at the start of the day, but the 'real' them will usually show through by the end of the day.

It is always a help to have a second opinion on your preferred candidate: a colleague or adviser may be able to spot something you haven't noticed before, or just confirm that you are on the right lines. Why not:

- Have one or two team members sit in on the interviews.
- Let the team decide which person they would prefer to work with.
- Ask the final two applicants to do a presentation to you and the team.

Select whom you believe to be the best candidate and consider setting up a probationary period — three months is the normal length of time. That will give you *and* them the opportunity to get to know each other better. However, during that period if the person is not performing you will need to go through the same performance discussions as you would with a permanent employee. You cannot, at the end of a probationary period, suddenly dismiss the person with no notice. Even during the probationary period, you must have conducted the process in a procedurally correct manner. Since October 2004, all employers in the UK have a legal obligation to set out disciplinary and dismissal rules in writing; if you attempt to fire an employee without having followed these procedures, you will automatically be deemed as having dismissed that person unfairly.

It's essential that you are aware of all relevant legislation when you recruit someone: saying that you 'didn't know' about it won't get you far when you're being sued. The Acas website (www.acas.org.uk) has a helpful overview of the process, and you could also take professional legal advice if you have any queries or concerns.

Step 8 After the interviews

Always let people know the outcome of the interviews as quickly as possible — preferably within seven days. Not letting unsuccessful applicants know you have made a selection decision is an area where companies often fall down.

It is worth remembering that unsuccessful candidates are a bit like customers: if they are not treated well, they'll make sure as many people as possible hear about it.

Step 9 Checking references

A high percentage of CVs contain misstatements of fact. And it is estimated that 69% of organisations claim to perform some sort of check on potential employees, yet we frequently hear about bogus directors or fraudulent

CEOs. How many people find out after they've employed someone that, if only they'd checked references first, they wouldn't have touched the candidate with a barge pole!

Always ask the interviewee for permission to contact referees. It is perfectly normal, however, for an interviewee to ask you not to contact their current employer. A word of caution: on one occasion I interviewed a person with excellent written references but who simply refused to provide any verbal referees at all. Needless to say, I went no further with that person. They may have been absolutely genuine, but I simply would not risk employing anyone without a verbal reference check.

You will also need to check university degrees. Nowadays there are numerous reported instances where people have faked their qualifications; there are also many disreputable agencies who guarantee never to fail anyone on their courses. If the qualification is mandatory to the position, you must check that it is bona fide and of a high standard. It is also important that you check whether overseas qualifications are of an acceptable quality and valid in the United Kingdom.

TIP 19

Look at the whole picture.

Believe it or not, some people nominate relatives as referees. This is a bad sign in itself! Don't be afraid to ask what the interviewee's relationship is with the people they have nominated if you have any doubts.

Ask the employee for a minimum of three referees. Depending on the position you are seeking to fill, at the very least, you will want to talk to a previous manager, a peer and a subordinate. If you're recruiting a new manager or supervisor and your chosen candidate doesn't have any experience of that type of role thus far, you should talk to two previous managers, one of whom has observed the person working.

If the preferred candidate for a management position does have some experience of that role, speak to someone who has observed them dealing with staff, and to someone they have managed.

Ask the prospective employee for the names and contact details of their referees. You cannot contact anyone they have not nominated. When you come to speak to the referees, ask some of the following:

Openers
- What was/is your professional relationship to the applicant?
- Did you have an opportunity to observe the actual performance of the person?

■ How were you able to do that and how often?

Checking the employee's skill-base

■ We are looking for someone with good computer literacy. How would you rate this person in this area?

■ Time management is important in this position. In your opinion, did this person display good skills in this area?

Check attitudinal criteria

■ Occasionally our receptionist is required to help other departments when they get busy. How flexible did you find this person?

Also always check the tenure and final salary — these are the two areas people are most likely to exaggerate.

And the $64,000 question you must always ask is:

■ Would you re-employ this person?

When you have asked that question, listen very carefully. Listen for a long pause (this could be an indication that the person is trying to work out what to say without getting into stormy waters). Listen for an intake of breath (ditto). Also, listen for the tone they use when answering. All these could be clues to a referee who is wary of saying too much.

Asking for proof of qualifications and identity

Asking for proof of qualifications possibly won't be something a potential employer would be comfortable doing. However, it is certainly something recruitment agencies must undertake to do.

I am based in New Zealand, and there was a recent example of this situation there. A man called John Davy, who was hired as head of Maori TV, would never had got that job if the recruitment agency had had checks in place with regard to qualifications. The university he supposedly gained his qualifications from did not, in fact, exist.

If they had ever bothered to check his references, they would also have discovered a man who had travelled the world, leaving behind him a trail of failed businesses — not the sort of person you would want to head a company responsible for millions of tax-payers' dollars.

And if asking for proof of qualifications proves difficult, imagine having to ask for proof of identity!

A recent case came to light of an employee defrauding a New Zealand government department of $2 million over three years, a situation which also could have been avoided had a more rigorous checking system been in place. Once again, even though this employee was recruited by a reputable agency, the agency had failed to ask for any proof of identity. It was subsequently discovered that not only had this person falsified her name and date of birth when applying for the position, she also had criminal convictions for dishonesty-related offences and had twice been declared a bankrupt.

Unfortunately, we live in a world where we can no longer take people at face value. Checking references and qualifications, and asking for proof of identity is now vital. Finding out after the event is too late.

Step 10 Evaluating the process

Once a new person is in place, we are often so busy bringing them up to speed and picking up on all the jobs that piled up while we were recruiting, that we rarely take the time to evaluate the recruitment process itself.

If you regularly assess the new recruit throughout the three-month probationary period, it is a simple matter to factor in an evaluation of the process used at the same time. This could be done in one of two ways.

1. **Talk to the person's team leader (if it's not you!) — ask how things went for them, and if they are happy with the outcome.**

2. Involve the whole team, including the new recruit. Obviously this is not the time to talk about the person's performance, merely the process. But I would also ask the new recruit — separately — how the process went for them and what improvements could be made.

Questions to ask are:

- What went well?
- What didn't go so well?
- What did we do that we perhaps should not have done?
- What did we not do that we should have?

This may all seem a very lengthy and convoluted process, but these are two-minute conversations, really. It is important to evaluate the process while it is fresh in people's minds. Six months down the track, everyone will have forgotten any good ideas they had for improvement. Remember, mistakes are costly.

PART IV

Recruiting at team leader and management level

People don't leave organisations, they leave managers!

WHAT ARE YOU: MANAGER OR LEADER?

Do you consider yourself a leader or a manager? And what exactly is the difference anyway?

When you run your own business, you have to wear lots of 'hats', especially in the early days when there's so much to do, but not always many people around to help. As your business matures and expands, though, the difference between managers and leaders does become more pronounced and you'll have to think about how best to look after your staff and who, in the cold light of day, is the best person to do it. It might not be you any more. For example:

- Managers tend to think of themselves as the 'boss'.
- Leaders tend to think of themselves as coaches and mentors.

- Managers tend to follow rules to the letter and expect everyone else to do the same.
- Leaders tend to use the rules as a guideline only and are always looking for creative and more efficient ways of doing things. The leader's attitude tends to be, 'Let's review and change the rules if that seems to be the best way forward.'
- Managers usually want to make all the decisions themselves, whereas leaders will consciously involve their teams in making decisions because they know that when people are included they are more likely to make sure that decisions are implemented.
- If things go wrong (as they often do), managers tend to find someone to blame; leaders take the responsibility themselves, and then go back to find the reason.
- Managers are prone to hoard information because information is power; leaders tend to share as much information as is appropriate. How will people know whether they are doing a good job or not if they don't have the information to make an assessment?

Some questions to ask yourself

- Is there high turnover in your business?
- Do you know what the average length of tenure actually is in a typical job at your company?
- If turnover is high, are you willing to find out why?
- If turnover is high, what needs to be changed before a new person joins so they don't end up leaving after six months?

If it's even remotely possible that you are the reason why people are leaving your organisation, you will need to do whatever it takes to address the problem. It is painful, yes, but you have to put the business first.

Team leader assessment

Answer the following questions and rate yourself as follows:

- 5 = always
- 4 = most of the time
- 3 = some of the time
- 2 = rarely
- 1 = never

1. I listen openly and carefully to what others have to say.
2. I encourage others to share ideas and opinions.
3. I set clear performance expectations.
4. I give regular feedback to others on their performance.
5. I provide others with opportunities to learn and grow.
6. I treat staff with respect and dignity.
7. I involve others in decisions which affect them.
8. I share information and knowledge with others.
9. I support and encourage staff to advance.
10. I hold regular team meetings.

Ask your team for feedback on how they would rate you!

Recruiting at the team leader level

The 'supervisor'

A long-term employee of a company worked his way up to be what he called 'a working foreman'. He ruled by absolute fear. He shouted at everyone, he was racist, he didn't believe in having meetings with his own people and rarely attended branch meetings. His philosophy was that meetings were a waste of time and that, while he was in meetings, he wasn't getting product out the door.

He hated being sent on training, and resisted sending his staff on training. Quite simply, he hated being away from his department because, in his words, 'I can't watch what my lazy scum-bags [employees] are doing.' He did, however, get the product out to customers.

The problem? He got product out of the door at a huge cost. The staff under his supervision (rather than under his leadership) were never encouraged to think, to contribute or to grow. One team member had worked on the same machine for eight years; he was a bright man, perfectly capable of learning other aspects of the production process.

With supervisors or managers who treat people this way, some hard questions have to be asked and some tough calls have to be made.

85

The company was reluctant to tackle him because he presented one of those challenges that went into the 'too-hard' basket. His manager preferred to leave things as they were, knowing that the man was close to retirement. Yet, as people often want to (or have to) work past the traditional retirement age, he could have been with the company for a good few years yet. And when he finally did retire, what would he have left behind and what damage would he have caused? By his way of running the department, he was ensuring that people would never acquire the skills or the confidence to run the department in his absence. This probably suited him; it meant that no-one would ever be better than him. No successor had ever been nominated because everyone was too scared to broach the subject, and meanwhile some very bright people left.

It is important to look for team leaders and managers who have the self-esteem to allow people around them to grow, so that when they do leave there is a smooth transition and productivity remains high — regardless of who the team leader might be.

TIP 20

A coach's role is to have people see what they would rather not see, hear what they would

> rather not hear, so they can become the person they always suspected they could become.

Internal promotion

So far we have explored questions for recruiting staff at the front end of an organisation. The higher we go in the organisation, the more skilled people are at being interviewed, hence the more skilled employers need to be in asking the right questions.

Career development is important. It's a good idea to advertise jobs internally, and be creative in the way you do it. Many organisations advertise their vacancies online, forgetting that some applicants may not have access to a computer, or the skills to use one. Yet these very people may be the raw material you can use to start growing the business.

When interviewing internal candidates for a promotional position, there are two basic mistakes that are often made:

1. We promote our best widget-maker, salesperson or computer analyst to team leader or manager. By doing this we often lose out on two fronts – not only do we lose our

best salesperson (or widget-maker) but we 'gain' a lousy manager or team leader, because people need very different skills to be a manager or team leader.

2. We see the person *only* as a widget-maker or salesperson and fail to see that they have other skills.

When seeking team leaders (as opposed to supervisors) we need to look for a completely different skills set:

1. leadership skills
2. people and conflict-resolution skills
3. communication skills
4. the ability to analyse productivity problems
5. judgement — knowing when to step forward and when to step back
6. meeting and negotiation skills
7. planning and organisation skills
8. technical and/or business translation skills
9. political awareness
10. the ability to 'sell' unpopular changes to the team
11. the ability to motivate people to get better results
12. a desire to develop people

13. delegation skills
14. creativity – the ability to constantly find ways to do more with less – which is an incredibly tall order!

Recruiting at the middle/senior management level

At the senior management level, people need all of the previous skills plus:

- a vision which is communicated, gets buy-in and inspires
- global/strategic thinking
- decisiveness
- the courage to make the hard decisions and, when necessary, to take risks
- facilitation skills
- entrepreneurial skills
- market awareness
- sound ethics
- a system for analysing day-to-day results while keeping an eye on the future
- the ability to appraise complex situations quickly and effectively
- decision analysis and completion
- mentoring skills

- the self-confidence to employ people who are better than them
- the willingness to identify and develop their successors

Use questions which identify real-life scenarios (something they are likely to encounter on the job). For example:

> You have an incredibly tight deadline and it is obvious the department is not going to make it. Talk me through what you would do.

Remember to give the same scenario to everyone you interview for the position.

When recruiting anyone, cultural fit with the organisation is vital. Culture is simply 'the way we do things around here'. Often, when a good culture of communication and trust has been built between a team and their manager, that manager leaves and a new one is recruited. If the new person has not been recruited to work within the team culture, their first reaction is often: 'Well, you can just forget all that warm fuzzy stuff!' And so the whole process is lost and employees become cynical about working as a team!

> **TIP 21**
>
> A manager's job is to do him- or herself out of a job within a two- to five-year period.

Psychometric testing – to do or not to do?

Psychometric testing is a tool that is strongly recommended for anyone who is moving into a management position. Psychometric tests can elicit information which is difficult to obtain any other way. They remove bias and prejudice, and they can be very useful in finding a team 'fit'.

Michael Gerber, author of *The E Myth*, talks about three distinct working styles:

1. the technician who likes doing the doing
2. the manager, who likes working with the systems, and
3. the entrepreneur, who constantly searches for more creative ways to do things.

Technicians are not what is needed at the management level – that's the kind of thinking which contributes to the mistake of promoting the best salesperson. Selling is a 'technician' skill.

Managers therefore need to be good at either creating systems or improving systems; at the senior level, it is absolutely essential that they have entrepreneurial skills – and are constantly challenging the status quo.

The right type of psych tests will also reveal a person's preferred style of leadership:

1. **autocratic (like the supervisor earlier)**
2. **laissez-faire (avoiding the hard decisions, burying their head in the sand and hoping things will go away)**
3. **democratic (what we need in today's workplace – the type of people who involve others in decision making)**

However, if you do decide to use psych testing, never base a hiring decision on the results of this alone. Remember, it is only a tool. It is still advisable to use traditional methods. At the senior management level it is certainly recommended that a person be interviewed by several different people.

Never rush a recruitment decision at any level, but particularly at the middle or senior level. Golden parachutes can be very expensive.

The use of professional recruitment agencies

Professional recruitment agencies are like any other professional bodies – there are good ones and there are mediocre ones. Once you have built a good relationship with a reputable agency, there are two powerful ways you can use their services:

1. Determine the shortlist yourself, then pay the agency to run the final one or two candidates through a few targeted aptitude tests.
2. Do the exact opposite and have the agency conduct the preliminary interviews and bring their shortlist to you.

The first way is the cheaper option, but either way, by involving a third party you will save yourself a considerable amount of time and gain additional and objective back-up data on which to make your final selection.

PART V

SUMMARY

DOS AND DON'TS DURING THE INTERVIEW

Do:

- set the scene so that people feel at ease
- give people a few minutes to settle down
- give them a chance to talk for a large part of the interview
- listen (and hear)
- ask 'open' questions, ie those that can't be answered with just 'yes' or 'no'
- be up to date with all relevant employment legislation: if you're not sure, find out *before* the interview

Don't:

- assume anything – if in doubt, ask, and if you have a concern, check!

- over-glamorise the position
- hog the conversation – this is not about you
- use the interview process as a power trip

Encourage creative applications

If you are in the fortunate position of owning or managing a company where jobs are in great demand, you will need to ask prospective employees to apply in a creative way, otherwise you will find yourself knee-deep in CVs.

A newly created position with a radio station was bound to attract an avalanche of applications. A woman who desperately wanted to break into radio but had no experience, apart from some background in amateur drama, knew she would have to do something pretty spectacular to be interviewed. She went to a studio and had an audiotape made of her voice, then duly sent the audio, tied to a helium balloon, to the radio station. She was not only successful in gaining an interview, she actually got the job!

An American food company asks prospective recruits to sing their favourite song – not to see if the applicant can sing, but to see if they have the courage to step out of their comfort zone, are inventive, and (perhaps) have the ability to laugh at themselves. And another US company asks prospective employees to write an essay on the oldest piece of clothing in their wardrobe.

> **TIP 22**
>
> We all love to talk about ourselves. The secret of a good interviewer is to create a space for candidates to do this. After all, what will you learn about the other person if you do all the talking?

Conducting exit interviews

Never assume you know why people are leaving your company. Always be gracious enough to ask — and be willing to hear the answer.

People rarely leave an organisation just because of money. They may say this is the reason they are leaving — they may even think it is — but usually, money is simply the final straw. Their dissatisfaction has usually been brewing for quite some time before they make the final decision to go.

Having said that, it is important to know the market rate for your key positions. When there's worldwide demand for workers, rest assured the headhunters are out in force, and if you have fallen behind in your rates for certain positions, they will use that as a powerful lever to encourage good people to leave.

> **TIP 23**
>
> The happiest people don't necessarily have the best of everything, they just make the most of whatever comes their way.

Over the years I have witnessed two phenomena:

- employees who were poached by companies offering them a larger salary package than their existing employer, returned after six to eight months because they hated the atmosphere of the new organisation.
- employees who were given more money to stay, still left after six months because the extra money appeased them only for a little while, until the real reasons they were miserable surfaced again.

Remember, it was from interviews with the tele-marketers who were leaving in droves that we realised we were recruiting the wrong people and advertising the wrong job. We would never have discovered that if we hadn't asked people why they were leaving — and made it safe for them to tell us.

These interviews must be conducted after people have had their final pay and after they have received their references. Preface this discussion with a disclaimer stating that the information you are gathering is to discover why people are leaving, and whether there is anything that can be done to address those reasons. In particular, stress that the information the employee gives you will not be held against them.

Never lose sight of the time and money involved in replacing an existing employee.

Some questions to ask:

- Are you leaving to take up another position?
- Is the position similar or very different from this one?
- What worked well for you here?
- Which areas do you feel we could improve in?
- What were the factors which contributed to your decision to leave?

It is useful, when a person does decide to leave, to raise the issue at your regular team meeting. Ask co-workers if they know any relevant details, and how it could have been prevented. Once again, this is not about blame or snitching, it is about avoiding losing any more valuable people.

Creative ways around the people shortage

A supermarket in New Zealand was having great difficulty in finding new recruits and, given that the industry traditionally has a high turnover of staff, knew they had to do something different.

They made a conscious decision to recruit highly qualified new immigrants who were having difficulty getting a start in their preferred line of work. They knew that most of these people wouldn't stay long once they had some New Zealand work experience behind them, but they also realised that during their short stay they would probably add immense value simply because of their higher-than-average intelligence. Miracle of miracles, some of these applicants were actually persuaded to stay with the company to pursue a career in the food industry.

If you can get past the concern that some people won't stay forever, and accept the fact that along the way some movers and shakers may challenge the status quo; and if you can see this as a positive thing rather than a negative thing, they could pay for themselves tenfold.

Be willing to occasionally stretch your own thinking.

Above all else, don't stifle any of your employees. Encourage people; give them space, watch them grow and then watch your profits grow.

Keep key CVs on file

If you have just interviewed some bright people who are not absolutely right for the position you are advertising but who have impressed you, then hang onto their information. Remember to ask their permission first.

Your chosen candidate may not work out. If you have kept their application details you will then be able to contact your second choice candidate. Often, another job will come up and you will be able to use these CVs as your starting point in the search for applicants. It regularly saved me having to go through the whole recruiting process all over again.

If you have two exceptional candidates, see if you can find a placement for the second person in another department. In an industry with high turnover, you may have a surplus person for a while, but within a very short space of time someone else will leave and you already have a replacement.

Retaining your new employees

You have found your wonderful new employee: now what? Let me tell you a story . . .

Once upon a time there was an ethical consultant. All her working life she had been honest and acted with total integrity. When she died and arrived at the Pearly Gates, she found St Peter scratching his head. He had never encountered an ethical consultant before and didn't quite know what to do with her. After much deliberation he decided to be creative and offer her one day in Hell and one day in Heaven and then let her decide for herself where she wanted to spend Eternity.

The first day she went down in the lift to Hell. It was like nothing she had ever imagined. It was so beautiful. Everywhere she looked she saw parks and rivers and exquisite trees. She met up with all her old consultant friends who were better dressed than she had ever seen them when they were alive. They were laughing and joyful and she spent the most wonderful day with them.

She spent the next day in Heaven and it, too, was very nice. She had a peaceful and relaxing day, though she didn't run into any of her old colleagues.

And then she had to report to St Peter with her final decision.

She told him that, as lovely as she found Heaven, she had made the decision to move to Hell because all her friends were there, and they were having such a marvellous time together.

And so her wish was granted. This time, however, when the lift doors opened, she found a very different Hell. She saw it was hot, filthy and dark. All her old friends rushed to greet her, but now they were dressed in rags. Waiting there to greet was the Devil himself.

'What happened,' she cried? 'Where are all the beautiful surroundings and what happened to my well-dressed colleagues?'

'Ah,' the Devil replied. 'Yesterday was recruitment day, today you're staff!'

Once you have found your amazing new recruit with the fabulous attitude and all the skills you required, don't abandon them. Finding great people is only a small part of the employee equation; you now have to find a way to retain them.

> **TIP 24**
>
> Training increases productivity by about 20%. Training accompanied by coaching, follow-up and feedback increases productivity by approximately 90%.

Think back to those times when you took on a new job. Was there an induction programme or were you just left to work things out for yourself? Were you given a buddy or a mentor, someone to look after you during that first week or so, or were you left to get on with it alone? Did anyone sit with you at regular intervals during your first three months to tell how you were progressing, or were you kept in the dark and left to guess?

Induction, mentoring and regular performance appraisals must be put in place for any new person. Don't put all that time and effort into selecting the best people for your organisation, only to abandon them once they're in.

> **TIP 25**
>
> Make performance appraisals a two-way process. Be brave enough to ask:

- What do I do as your manager that you appreciate?
- What could I do differently to make our working relationship more effective ?

Giving and receiving feedback

Many companies have been experimenting with two-way feedback (sometimes also referred to as '360 degree feedback'). The intent is honourable; it is empowering to allow people the opportunity to give and receive feedback on their performance, and to be able to do the same for their manager.

Unfortunately, the results are not always great. One organisation has a regular internal customer survey which gives employees an opportunity to rate their managers and the company. Basically this has turned into a 'shredding' exercise, and it has left some of the managers involved feeling deeply wounded and powerless because they don't always know who has said what, or how to put things right.

TIP 26

Managers need courage. They also need to be careful about being too careful!

Because receiving feedback is a fairly nerve-wracking experience for both parties, an excellent way to get such sessions off to a good start is to give only positive feedback in the first two or three sessions. It is amazing how people respond to praise. Obviously this needs to be genuine praise; with some people it is difficult to find anything positive to say, but no matter how hard it is, give it a try. Everyone has some strengths or skills.

Once employees are over the initial nervousness of the process, it is then possible to add 'And one thing you could do to improve is . . .'

Even more courageous is to give employees permission to give you, their manager, some feedback too. Use the same process: ask them to give you only positives for, say, the first two or three sessions, then once each party feels ready, add the one thing they need you to do differently for them.

The employee/manager relationship can be improved beyond all recognition if both parties are willing to sit down together and give honest and open feedback to each other. Neither party is a mind-reader. If the employee is unaware of what they are doing (or not doing) to be more productive, then how will they learn. And if you, as their manager, don't know what they need from you to help them improve their productivity, how will you learn? People are lousy mind-readers.

How about practising this face-to-face feedback at your next performance appraisals? You could also ask the teams for feedback on your management style. They will tell you if you make it OK for them to do that.

You will never please everyone. And that isn't actually the aim when you are in a leadership role. However, you are charged with the bottom-line results, and if you keep losing people because you are either being too harsh or too soft on them, then you are failing at your job.

Most employees want managers who are firm but fair, who are willing to make the hard decisions whether they are people decisions or bottom-line decisions.

The importance of performance appraisals

Traditionally, most organisations conduct annual performance appraisals. Some confess to never doing them, which is a tragedy. It begs the question again, if people don't know what they are doing wrong, how will they ever get it right?

The biggest reason managers give for not conducting regular appraisals is time. They claim they're too busy and complain that the appraisals simply take too long to do.

> It is vital that managers should get past this way of thinking. Performance appraisals need to be conducted every two to three months rather than annually.
>
> The more communication that managers have with their employees, the more they are able to give them feedback and direction, the faster employees improve and the greater their output. Time spent In appraisals is not a waste of management time, it is the most important use of their time.

Become an employer of choice

Before I start working with a team, I send every team member a questionnaire which is to be filled out in the strictest confidence and returned directly to me. It is my way of finding out what is really going on in a team.

One of the questions I ask is: Which is one organisation in New Zealand you really admire? Popular answers are The Warehouse (a large retailer similar to Woolworth's), Hubbard Foods (breakfast cereal maker) and Fisher & Paykel (a kitchen products stockist).

The next question is, of course: Why do you admire them? The typical responses are:

- They look after their employees.
- They care about their customers.
- They seem to care about the environment and their local community.
- They give the impression that they are not just about the bottom line.
- They support various local charities.

Maybe they do and maybe they don't; perception isn't always reality. Bill Gates found out in the early days of Microsoft that the *perception* of working for his organisation was so great, he had a never-ending supply of potential recruits.

What is the perception of your organisation in the marketplace? And if you don't know, would you like to find out? All you have to do is conduct internal and external surveys.

Conduct regular internal/external customer surveys

External client surveys are now fairly commonplace. The hope is that, once an organisation has received some feedback from its customers, it will actually do something about that feedback.

Organisations or companies could also benefit from asking their employees what they would like from the organisation. Ask what people want and they will tell you. You may not be able to provide everything, but your employees will be encouraged that you even asked. And you may learn something.

PART VI

Planning for the future

The illiterate of the [new] millennium will not be those who can't read or write, but those who can't learn, unlearn and relearn.

Alvin Toffler

PART VI

Planning for the future

CREATE A CAREER DEVELOPMENT POLICY

No matter what the industry — manufacturing, IT, you name it — the thinking is the same: if no one expects the workers to grow, they don't. Sure, if someone really stands out, notice is taken, but for the majority of people, unless they do something absolutely outstanding, they are basically left to rot in their own little corner of the world.

Even today, with a worldwide shortage of good, skilled labour, most companies do not consider career development for general staff. We can't treat our employees this way any longer, though. If you don't have their long-term interests at heart (which, at the end of the day, are actually your own interests) you will lose the good ones. It is as simple as that.

Make it easy for people to grow.

A really smart career development tool is to adopt the 'each one teach one' school of learning. Once an employee becomes proficient at what they do, ask them what one thing they would like to learn. In order to create space for them to be able to do that, what one thing can they teach someone else?

TIP 27

If you don't look after your people, someone else will!

You could create an organisation or department where, for two hours every month, people are either learning something new or teaching something to someone else.

Part of the one-to-one sessions could also include the following questions:

1. How can we help you grow and develop?
2. What are your two- and five-year goals?
3. What skills do you believe you need to get you there?
4. What are the current gaps in your skills?
5. How can we help you achieve your goals?
6. What are you willing to hand over (and teach) someone else, so you can free up your time to take on new tasks?

This is not to say that the organisation should pay for all the development a person may need. You could be creative and set up a process to reimburse the fees on successful completion of a course. Or you could organise a 50/50 split in the fees between the company and the employee. Successful career development should be based on the employee having to make a substantial effort. Spoon feeding is not a good way to create a learning, growing organisation.

One company has an employee programme called 'Dream Catcher'. After three years' service, and at the beginning of the year, each employee lets someone know what their 'dream' is for the year. If, for example, the employee aims to save for a holiday or a new car, the company promises to match whatever the employee saves towards that dream. This is, in the end, much cheaper that the cost of recruiting new people.

Give people as much autonomy as they can handle. Teach people how to make quality decisions. Coach them rather than fire them if they make a bad decision. After all, how did you as a manager learn to make good decisions? Probably by making a lot of mistakes along the way.

Watch for early warnings of people being unsettled and looking elsewhere. At this early stage you can possibly discover what is not working for them and rescue the situation.

Conduct regular one-on-ones

I was coaching a team leader in how to do performance appraisals with his team. This was the first time he had ever conducted appraisals himself and it was the first time the organisation had ever taken appraisals to the factory-floor level.

We had successfully interviewed five members of his team and were sitting waiting for the next employee when the team leader said, 'The next person coming to join us is the slowest person in my team!'

We started the appraisal in exactly the same way we had with all the previous employees, the team leader telling the employee what he was doing well and suggesting one or two areas where he could improve. Then the team leader actually said: 'You are the slowest person on the line.'

The employee, almost leaping from his seat, responded with: 'No I'm not, you just keep putting me in the wrong place. You keep putting me on as pacesetter and I can't do that, I find it too stressful; but if you put me second in the line, I can keep up with anyone in this team!'

We all sat in stunned silence for a moment. Then we

realised we had just learned something very powerful —
the biggest lesson anyone in a management position
can learn: never assume anything. Always check.

The next day, the employee was placed exactly
where he said he needed to be. He was happy, the line
went smoothly; the team was happy and the team
leader was ecstatic.

Make jobs interesting

If you are not sure how to make sure people's jobs are
interesting, ask them during the one-to-one what they
would like to learn in order to grow. Ask them what their
ambitions are, what excites them. They will tell you.

It is every manager's role to allow people to grow,
and you can only do that if you talk to your employees
regularly. Get to know them as people, not just as lab
technicians, computer programmers or receptionists.

When you are conducting your appraisals you also
have the opportunity to ask employees why they stay
with the organisation. You may find some surprises.

Often, in the absence of on-the-job stimulation, you
will find many people stay because of their friendships
with co-workers, or because the hours suit their out-of-
work activities. If your employees stay because of
reasons like these, rather than having a career plan,
then sooner or later they will leave for greener pastures.

Holding onto the best employees

Retaining good staff is a problem in most organisations. Employers are going to have to be a lot more creative to retain staff in the future. They may even have to think differently: instead of matching people to jobs, they will have to look at matching jobs to people.

There is a very high turnover of women in the corporate world. Most women will at some stage think about starting a family and, if their current position doesn't encourage that, then they will leave. Men are increasingly choosing to be involved in bringing up their children – they, too, are demanding more flexible work hours.

TIP 28

Ask people why they stay with your organisation.

The concept of job sharing has been around for a long time; many organisations encourage it and have found it works. And with the sophistication of today's technology, a great number of people now work from home. The employer's fear is that they won't be working, but doing the gardening or out shopping. The test is in the results they achieve (or not).

Some people prefer to work at night rather than during the day. Set the targets and define the responsibilities of the job, then allow employees to choose how, when and where they do the work. If they are not performing, deal with the performance issue. Treat people as adults and, hopefully, they will respond as adults.

Set exciting team goals

If you can get people to participate and have them clearly understand what their role is in the process, you can set some ambitious objectives for them and more often than not, they achieve and sometimes exceed their goals.
Ralph Norris in *The Hero Manager*, Brad Jackson & Ken Parry

Keeping up with the speed of change should never be thought of as purely a management challenge. *Everyone* in an organisation should be encouraged to keep an eye on what is happening in the marketplace, to observe great ideas, to be aware of gaps in the market and to experience excellent customer service in action. They should be encouraged to bring those ideas and observations back to the organisation, asking the question 'How can we use that idea to add value to this business?'

Then they should be given permission and space to apply those ideas.

As we mentioned in Part II, employees constantly complain about shifting goalposts, yet it is vital for them to understand that because of the speed of change in the business world today, shifting the goalposts regularly is not only a very positive thing, it can be a life-saving thing. Once employees grasp this reality, they are usually only too keen to put forward ideas to help the business stay afloat. After all, they have a vested interest in its survival.

Organisations who fail to stay alert to ever-increasing customer expectations and advances in technology, or who tire of regularly developing new products and services, are at risk of being left behind — or even becoming obsolete!

Involve people and you will be amazed at the energy that is released. Ignore people and they become robots. Most people would dearly love to leap out of bed every morning, wanting to get to work. The reality is, that such energy and passion is rare. Managers blame employees for being apathetic and employees blame managers for never listening. The answer lies in the two parties communicating and working together as adults who want the organisation they work for to be successful.

Set up cross-functional, multi-disciplined, brainstorming teams and watch the sparks fly. Reward people for great ideas and they will bring more ideas than you can handle. Which challenge would you rather have — apathetic employees or too many ideas to implement?

Create an ongoing learning culture

Many organisations have created a culture which says, the only way to earn more around here is to learn more. No one needs to be confused about the learning culture of such an organisation.

The average cost of training and development in any organisation should be around 2% of the wage and salary bill. How much are you spending on growing your people? It is a very basic litmus test. If you are spending more, that's great, but if you are spending less, then your non-learning culture could cost you down the track.

In *Hiring and Keeping the Best People*, Harvard Business Essentials suggest that you can expect a 1:33 return on your investment. So for every pound spent on training, you can expect a £33 return through improved productivity. Why wouldn't you train your staff?

Succession planning and beyond

Part of the role of a senior manager is to do themselves out of a job within a two- to five-year framework.

It is not healthy for people to get into a management

position and then become 'corporate concrete' – that's someone who has grown to the upper level of their competence and decides to coast it out to retirement. If a senior manager is not growing, then you can be sure the people they manage will not be encouraged to grow either.

It may be that no-one in your organisation is yet ready to take on your position, but if you don't know whether they're keen to develop, how can you help them grow? And if you don't let them know what the gaps are in their development, how can they do something about being ready the next time a position becomes available?

Look also at key team members. Who are the most skilled in your team and how vulnerable would you be if they left? Who is being groomed to take over their role? Who else could fill the gap, even temporarily, if they were to have a heart attack or a road accident?

As an organisation you may have the best product in the world, the best technology in the world, the best distribution systems ever invented, but if you don't recruit and retain the best people you will only ever be second best. However, if you are willing to invest in finding and keeping the best people you will be well on the way to being world class.

Zig Ziglar, well-known motivator, once said: 'There's only one thing more frustrating that training employees and having them leave, and that is not training them and having them stay.'

No organisation has any product or service that their competitors don't already have, or won't have within a very short space of time. The only competitive advantage any organisation has is its people.

SOURCES

Andrews, Ann, *Shift Your But*. Ann Andrews, Auckland, 1997.

Compton, R.L., Morrissey, B. & Nankervis, A.R., *Effective Recruitment & Selection Practices*. CCH Australia, 2001.

Gerber, Michael E., *The E-Myth Revisited: Why Most Small Businesses Don't Work and What to Do About It*. Harper-Business, 1995.

Harvard Business Essentials, *Hiring and Keeping the Best People*. Harvard Business School Press, 2002.

Jackson, B. & Parry, K., *The Hero Manager*. Penguin, New Zealand, 2001.

Jay, Ros, *Brilliant Interview: What Employers Want to Hear and How to Say It*. Pearson Education, 2001.

Thompson, Carolyn B., *Interviewing Techniques for Managers*. McGraw-Hill, 2002.

INDEX

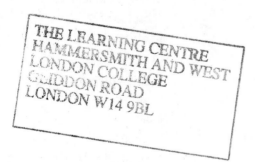